From 419 to Yahoo Yahoo

: *The Evolution of Internet Scams in Nigeria*

ABAYOMI ADEMOLA

Table of Contents

SHORT STORY ABOUT WHAT MOTIVATED THE AUTHOR

Abayomi Ademola was a common Nigerian citizen who had previously been duped by the famed 419 schemes. He had a traumatic encounter that made him feel defenseless and violated. But he didn't want to be a victim forever, so he chose to act independently.

To better understand how online frauds operate in Nigeria, Abayomi set out on a personal mission. He devoted numerous hours to his investigation, speaking with fraud victims, and even breaking into some of the most infamous online scamming networks. His objective was to reveal to the world the development of online scams in Nigeria.

Abayomi gained a lot of knowledge about the various scams throughout the years, from the traditional 419 schemes to the contemporary Yahoo Yahoo scams. He found that technology has greatly contributed to the growth of these con games, making it simpler for con artists to trick and control their victims.

Abayomi learned more about these scams' effects on Nigerian society as he dug deeper into his studies. The negative consequences included losses in money for people and businesses as well as a tarnished image of Nigeria abroad as a center for internet fraud.

Abayomi persevered despite the obstacles he encountered while conducting his research, including becoming the target of scammers and receiving threats for speaking out. To expose these frauds and assist others in avoiding becoming victims, he wrote the book "From 419 to Yahoo Yahoo: The Evolution Of Internet Scams in Nigeria."

Introduction

Internet scams have become a serious concern in Nigeria, with the nation being identified with a high frequency of these frauds. From the famed 419 scams to the development of Yahoo Yahoo, internet frauds have had a tremendous influence on Nigerian culture. However, the growth and history of these frauds are not commonly recognized, which is where this book, "From 419 to Yahoo Yahoo: The Evolution of Internet Scams in Nigeria," comes in.

The objective of this book is to offer readers a complete overview of the growth of online scams in Nigeria. The book analyzes the history of scams in Nigeria, including conventional scams and their shift to internet-based schemes. It also examines the birth of 419 schemes and their popularity in Nigeria, the advent of Yahoo Yahoo, and the influence of these frauds on Nigerian society.

This book is essential because it offers readers insights into a crucial social and economic issue in Nigeria. By exploring the impact of online fraud on individuals and the economy, the book provides light on the unfavorable repercussions of these scams. It also investigates the role of poverty and unemployment in the proliferation of online scams in Nigeria and the view of Nigeria as a hub for internet scams, which has had a detrimental influence on the country's reputation.

By reading this book, readers will obtain a better knowledge of the circumstances that contributed to the emergence of online scams in Nigeria and the problems of prosecuting internet fraudsters in the nation. The book also addresses the attempts of law enforcement to combat online fraud in Nigeria and the importance of international collaboration in the battle against these scams.

Overall, "From 419 to Yahoo Yahoo: The Evolution of Internet Scams in Nigeria" is a necessary read for anybody interested in understanding the growth of online scams in Nigeria and their influence on society. The book provides a detailed review of the history and growth of online scams in Nigeria and proposes feasible remedies to avoid their proliferation.

How It All Started

The word "419" refers to a form of scam that originated in Nigeria and is called after the part of the Nigerian penal code dealing with fraud. The Nigerian Prince fraud or Advance Fee Fraud are other names for the fraud.

It is impossible to determine who launched the 419 scams because it is said to have evolved from numerous sorts of Nigerian fraud schemes. However, it is widely assumed that it spread in Nigeria during the 1980s and 1990s when the country was experiencing economic difficulties and high unemployment rates. The first documented examples of 419 scams were related to Nigerian expatriates residing in the United States and Europe who attempted to swindle individuals out of their money through different tactics, such as bogus business agreements, inheritance scams, and bogus lottery victories.

The 419 scam is a sort of fraud in which a significant quantity of money is promised in exchange for a relatively little initial payment or investment. The scam generally begins with an unsolicited email or letter from a fraudster posing as a wealthy individual or business owner in need of assistance moving cash out of Nigeria or another country. The fraudster offers the victim a portion of the funds in exchange for their aid, but when the victim transfers the money, the scammer vanishes, leaving the victim with nothing.

The 419 scams have become well-known around the world, and it has been the topic of several news reports, documentaries, and even novels. It has also had a tremendous influence on Nigeria's and its people's reputation since the country has been connected with fraud for many years.

While the 419 scam's beginnings are unknown, it is said to have evolved from many forms of fraud schemes in Nigeria. According to one idea, the hoax may have evolved from the so-called "black money" scam, in which scammers claimed to have significant sums of cash dyed black to escape detection by customs officers. The fraudsters would then offer to sell the black money to victims, offering to wash the dye away and double or treble their investment.

The "wash-wash" fraud, which involved the use of chemicals to clear blackened US dollar notes, is another likely forerunner to the 419 scams. The fraudster would offer to sell the cleaned banknotes at a discount to the victim, claiming that they were worth much more than the reduced price.

Regardless of its beginnings, the 419 scams has become one of the world's most prevalent and profitable kinds of fraud. The FBI estimates that the fraud costs hundreds of millions of dollars each year, with victims from all walks of life and all corners of the globe.
Nigerian authorities have taken attempts in recent years to combat the 419 scam and other forms of fraud in the country. In 2003, the Economic and Financial Crimes Commission (EFCC) was formed to investigate and punish financial crimes, including 419 fraud. Although the government has had some success in apprehending and convicting fraudsters, the problem is still pervasive.

One explanation for the scam's continuous success is that it preys on its victims' gullibility and avarice. Scammers frequently persuade their victims that they are legitimate by employing convincing-sounding stories and documents, as well as playing on their aspirations and concerns. A scammer may, for example, pose as a wealthy businessman who needs assistance transferring money out of Nigeria to avoid paying taxes or to support a business endeavor. The fraudster may claim to split the earnings with the victim, but they will be required to pay numerous fees upfront to complete the deal.

To prevent being a victim of a 419 scam, be cautious of unsolicited emails or letters promising big quantities of money in exchange for a little upfront payment or investment. It is also critical to be wary of any offers that appear too good to be true, and to exercise caution when dealing with persons or corporations you do not know or trust. If you are approached by someone claiming to have a business or investment opportunity, do your homework and get advice from trustworthy people before making any choices or giving any money.

Chapter 1: The History of Scams in Nigeria

Scams have been a part of Nigerian society for decades, long before the arrival of the internet. These frauds were frequently carried out through face-to-face conversations, and they developed over time as new technology appeared. In this chapter, we will cover the history of scams in Nigeria, including their transfer to internet-based scams and the birth of 419 schemes.

Overview of the History of Scams in Nigeria

Nigeria has a long history of fraud, with many dating back to the colonial era. One of the earliest scams documented in Nigeria was the "wash-wash" scam in the 1960s, where fraudsters enticed victims to spend money in a program to wash black paper into real money. Another early scam was the "snake oil" scam, when fraudsters marketed phony medication and treatments to victims.

As technology progressed, so did the frauds. By the 1980s, the first telephone scams had evolved in Nigeria, when fraudsters induced victims to pay money for phony investment offers. The schemes continued to expand, and in the 1990s, the iconic 419 scams appeared.

The Emergence of 419 Scams

419 scams, also known as advance fee scams, are a kind of fraud where scammers promise victims a significant quantity of money in return for a small initial payment. The scams commonly comprise an email or letter that purports to be from a wealthy individual or a government figure who wants help moving cash out of the country.

The word "419" stems from the part of the Nigerian Criminal Code that deals with fraud. These frauds are rampant in Nigeria, and many people have fallen prey to them over the years. The scams have also moved to other nations, with numerous scammers working from Nigeria and other West African countries.

The Prevalence of 419 Scams in Nigeria

In Nigeria, 419 scams have become popular, with many fraudsters using the internet to carry out their schemes. The frauds have substantially impacted the country's economy and reputation, with many people equating Nigeria with fraud and scams.

The Nigerian government has taken steps to eliminate 419 frauds, yet they continue to be pervasive. Many victims have lost their life savings to these frauds, and the emotional toll on victims may be catastrophic.

The history of scams in Nigeria is a long and complex one, with many distinct forms of fraud growing throughout the years. The move from conventional scams to internet-based scams has been substantial, and the advent of 419 schemes has had a huge influence on Nigerian culture. While the Nigerian government has taken steps to counteract these frauds, they continue to be common, and many victims have suffered as a consequence.

Chapter 2: The Rise of Yahoo Yahoo

In the early 2000s, a new sort of online fraud arose in Nigeria, dubbed Yahoo Yahoo. It was called after Yahoo Messenger, one of the early internet chat programs that fraudsters used to contact their victims. The growth of Yahoo Yahoo coincided with the increased availability of internet connection and the development of cyber cafes in Nigeria.

Originally, Yahoo Yahoo was a relatively small-scale activity, largely carried out by individuals trying to earn quick money. But as the potential rewards expanded, organized criminal groups became engaged, resulting in a rapid increase in the volume and sophistication of the frauds.

Introduction to Yahoo Yahoo and its evolution in Nigeria

Yahoo is a sort of internet fraud that often includes impersonating a person or organization to fool the victim into handing over money or personal information. The scams can take numerous forms, such as bogus employment offers, inheritance scams, romance scams, and lottery scams, to mention a few.

Yahoo has changed dramatically over the years, with fraudsters getting more inventive and sophisticated in their efforts to dupe their victims. The frauds are now routinely carried out utilizing modern technology, including social engineering tactics, malware, and phishing assaults.

The importance of technology in the creation of Yahoo Yahoo scams

The increasing availability of technology has played a crucial influence in the emergence and development of Yahoo Yahoo scams in Nigeria. With access to the internet and other new technology, fraudsters have been able to reach a broader pool of victims and execute their hoaxes more successfully.

Social media sites like Facebook and Instagram have also become popular tools for fraudsters to interact with their victims. Scammers can construct bogus accounts and engage in chats with potential victims, frequently using sophisticated strategies to earn their confidence.

Examples of common Yahoo Yahoo scams and how they are implemented

One of the most popular Yahoo Yahoo scams is the "419 scam," called after the part of the Nigerian Criminal Code that deals with fraud. In this scam, the victim is generally approached by email or social media by someone claiming to be a wealthy Nigerian who needs help moving money out of the country. The fraudster will offer the victim a substantial proportion of the proceeds in exchange for their aid, but will eventually ask for money ahead to cover "processing fees" or other charges.

Another prevalent scam is the "romance scam," in which the fraudster establishes a bogus online profile on a dating site or social media platform and builds a connection with the victim. After winning the victim's confidence, the fraudster would beg for money for numerous reasons, such as a medical emergency or travel fees to meet in person.

Phishing scams are also widespread, in which the fraudster sends a false email or message that looks to be from a real entity, such as a bank or online shop. The message will often prompt the victim to click on a link and submit personal information, such as login credentials or credit card details.

In conclusion, the emergence of Yahoo Yahoo in Nigeria may be linked to a mix of circumstances, including the extensive availability of technology and the propensity of fraudsters to take advantage of vulnerable persons. While law enforcement organizations have taken efforts to crack down on Yahoo Yahoo scams, the scams continue to grow and adapt to new technology and strategies. It is crucial for individuals to be aware and careful while conversing online and to educate themselves about the hazards of online fraud.

Chapter 3: The Impact of Internet Scams on Nigerian Society

Internet frauds have had a tremendous influence on Nigerian society, impacting individuals, the economy, and the country's reputation. In this chapter, we will study the detrimental impacts of online scams on Nigerian society, the role of poverty and unemployment in the emergence of internet scams, and the reputation of Nigeria as a hub for internet scams.

The detrimental impact of online fraud on individuals and the economy

The impact of online fraud on individuals may be severe, both financially and emotionally. Victims of online fraud might lose their life savings, suffer from identity theft, and incur substantial psychological hardship. In addition, online frauds have a larger impact on the economy, including loss of income, decreased foreign investment, and harm to the reputation of Nigerian enterprises.

The Role of Poverty and Unemployment in the Rise of online scams in Nigeria

Poverty and unemployment are important contributing reasons to the emergence of online scams in Nigeria. With limited work options and high levels of poverty, many Nigerians turn to online scams as a method of generating money. The promise of quick and easy money might be enticing to persons trying to make ends meet, causing them to participate in unlawful activities.

The impression of Nigeria as a hotspot for online fraud and its influence on the country's reputation

The impression of Nigeria as a center for online fraud has had a considerable influence on the country's reputation, both locally and globally. The unfavorable reputation associated with online scams has led to increasing scrutiny of Nigerian firms and individuals, making it more difficult for reputable enterprises to build ties with overseas partners. In addition, the reputation of Nigeria as a country with high levels of fraud has had a detrimental impact on tourism and foreign investment.

The Nigerian government has made efforts to address the issue of online scams, including forming a specialized anti-fraud body, the Economic and Financial Crimes Commission (EFCC), and implementing laws to prevent internet fraud. However, the impact of online scams on Nigerian society remains enormous, and more has to be done to address the underlying problems contributing to the emergence of internet scams, such as poverty and unemployment.

In conclusion, the impact of online fraud on Nigerian society is considerable, harming individuals, the economy, and the country's reputation. Poverty and unemployment play a big part in the increase of online scams in Nigeria, underscoring the need for stronger efforts to address these underlying concerns. The Nigerian government and society as a whole must work together to combat online fraud and its harmful influence on Nigerian society.

Chapter 4: Law Enforcement and the Fight Against Internet Scams

Internet scams have become a serious concern in Nigeria, with numerous individuals and organizations falling prey to these fraudulent practices. Law enforcement authorities in Nigeria have been working relentlessly to prevent online fraud and bring those guilty to jail. In this chapter, we will analyze the obstacles to prosecuting online fraudsters in Nigeria, attempts by law enforcement to combat internet scams, and the significance of international collaboration in the battle against internet scams.

The Challenges of prosecuting online fraudsters in Nigeria

The prosecution of online fraudsters in Nigeria might be tough owing to various variables. One of the most serious difficulties is the paucity of resources available to law enforcement authorities. Many of these agencies are understaffed and lack the requisite tools to undertake complete investigations.

Another obstacle is the difficulty in tracking online frauds to their source. Many online fraudsters employ sophisticated tactics to mask their identity, making it tough to hunt them down. Additionally, the lack of assistance from foreign law enforcement authorities might make it hard to pursue crimes that have international aspects.

Efforts by law enforcement to combat online fraud in Nigeria

Despite the hurdles, law enforcement organizations in Nigeria have been working hard to prevent online fraud. The Economic and Financial Crimes Commission (EFCC)

has been in the vanguard of this endeavor, investigating and prosecuting cyber fraudsters across the country.

The EFCC has also initiated public awareness programs to educate the public about the hazards of online scams and how to prevent being a victim. Additionally, the EFCC has developed a Cybercrime Forensic Laboratory to aid in the investigation of internet fraud.

The Role of international collaboration in the Battle against
online frauds

International coordination is vital in the battle against internet fraud. Many online frauds are performed by people or groups operating outside Nigeria, making it tough to bring them to court. The EFCC has been collaborating with international law enforcement authorities to identify and prosecute cyber fraudsters.

In 2003, the EFCC signed a Memorandum of Understanding with the United States Federal Bureau of Investigation (FBI) to collaborate in the battle against online fraud. This partnership has resulted in the successful conviction of some high-profile internet crooks.

The EFCC has also struck similar agreements with law enforcement organizations in other nations, including the United Kingdom, Canada, and South Africa. These alliances have been vital in the battle against online fraud since they have permitted the exchange of information and resources across borders.

In conclusion, online fraud has become a big issue in Nigeria, harming individuals, businesses, and the country's reputation. Law enforcement authorities in Nigeria have been working relentlessly to prevent online fraud, but there are still big difficulties to be solved. International collaboration is vital in the battle against online fraud, and the EFCC has been cooperating with international law enforcement organizations to investigate and punish internet scammers.

Chapter 5: Current Methods Used by Internet Scammers in Nigeria and How to Protect Yourself

The growth of online scams in Nigeria has seen scammers create more complex tactics to deceive their victims. In this chapter, we will discuss some of the current strategies employed by online fraudsters in Nigeria and how you may defend yourself against them.

Phishing Scams: Phishing scams include scammers sending false emails or messages that appear to be from genuine sources, such as banks, social networking platforms, or online stores. These emails or messages generally contain links to bogus websites that appear like the actual ones, and unwary victims are fooled into inputting their personal and financial information. To protect yourself against phishing schemes, always double-check the URL before entering any personal information, and never click on strange links.

Lottery and Inheritance Scams: These scams include fraudsters calling their victims and saying that they have won a huge quantity of money in a lottery or inherited a significant amount of money from a distant relative. The fraudsters will ask for personal and financial details to process the wins or inheritance, but in reality, they are only attempting to steal the victim's identity or money. To prevent falling for these frauds, remember that authentic lotteries and inheritances do not need you to pay any fees ahead.

Business Email Compromise (BEC) Scams: BEC scams include criminals impersonating company leaders and sending bogus emails to workers or business partners to deceive them into transferring money or sensitive information. To defend yourself from BEC scams, always verify the validity of the email sender and double-check any demands for money or information.

Romance Scams: Romance scams involve scammers creating phony accounts on dating sites and other media platforms to mislead their victims into paying them money or revealing personal and financial information. To prevent falling for these scams, be aware of anyone who asks for money or tries to accelerate the connection too rapidly.

To safeguard oneself against online fraudsters, you should also:

- Keep your personal and financial information hidden and secure

- Use strong passwords and two-factor authentication
- Install and frequently update anti-virus and anti-malware software
- Stay updated on the current scams and frauds by periodically checking credible news sources and government websites

In conclusion, the rise of online scams in Nigeria has resulted in scammers utilizing increasingly complex tactics to deceive their victims. However, by remaining watchful and taking the proper steps, you may protect yourself from falling victim to these frauds.

What to Do If You Are a Victim of Internet Scams in the UK, Canada, and America.

Internet scams have become a global concern, and it is not unusual for individuals in the UK, Canada, and America to fall victim to these frauds. This chapter will cover what to do if you or someone you know has fallen victim to an internet scam in these nations.

What to do after becoming a victim:

If you or someone you know has fallen victim to an internet scam, it is crucial to act swiftly to limit the harm. Here are the steps you should take:

Contact your bank or financial institution immediately to report any fraudulent activities and to prohibit any future access to your accounts.

Change all your passwords and set up two-factor authentication for all your online accounts.

Report the incident to the relevant authorities in your country.

How to report scams in the UK: In the UK, you may report internet fraud to Action Fraud, the national fraud and cybercrime reporting center. You may report the fraud online, via phone, or by post.

How to report scammers in Canada: In Canada, you may report internet fraud to the Canadian Anti-Fraud Centre (CAFC). You may report the fraud online or by phone.

How to report scammers in America: In America, you may report online fraud to the Federal Trade Commission (FTC). You may report the fraud online, via phone, or by letter.

What to do if your family or friends become a victim:

If your relatives or friends fall prey to an internet scam, it is crucial to give them support and information. Here are some measures you may do to aid them:

Encourage them to report the fraud to the proper authorities.

Help them to change their passwords and set up two-factor authentication for their online accounts.

Advise them to be vigilant of any unsolicited calls, emails, or texts requesting personal or financial information.

In conclusion, falling prey to an internet scam can be an unpleasant experience, but it is crucial to respond swiftly to reduce the harm. By reporting the scam to the proper authorities and taking precautions to secure your online accounts, you can reduce the damage of the scam. Remember to also assist your relatives and friends who may fall prey to internet fraud, and educate them on the hazards of online fraud.

The Yahoo Yahoo scam is always changing, adapting to new technology and discovering new methods to take advantage of weak points in the system. As con artists discover new methods to take advantage of technology, the swindle is probably going to get much more complex in the future. The following are some major developments in the Yahoo Yahoo scam that we may anticipate in the future:

Artificial Intelligence (AI) and machine learning will be used increasingly frequently: As AI and machine learning develop, fraudsters will probably exploit these technologies to automate their activities. This may make it simpler for con artists to prey on huge numbers of unsuspecting people while simultaneously making it more challenging for law authorities to identify and stop their operations.

Greater emphasis on social engineering: A fundamental element of the Yahoo Yahoo scam is social engineering, and future fraudsters are likely to refine their methods even more. This can entail employing more specialized techniques, such as selecting victims based on their online activities and interests or utilizing deep fakes to produce more convincing frauds.

Increased usage of cryptocurrencies: Scammers are increasingly using cryptocurrencies as a tactic because they provide anonymous payment receipts and protection from law enforcement identification. Scammers are likely to use more sophisticated methods in the future to launder their money, such as decentralized exchanges or privacy currencies like Monero.

More individuals using mobile devices for banking and other financial operations will probably cause fraudsters to concentrate more on mobile platforms. This might entail utilizing SMS phishing assaults to choose victims or developing bogus mobile apps.

Increased collaboration among con artists: In recent years, there has been evidence of more collaboration among various con artist organizations, who exchange resources and knowledge to enhance their operations. As fraudsters search for new strategies to beat law enforcement, we may anticipate even more cooperation between various groups of con artists in the future.

What therefore can be done to prevent the Yahoo Yahoo fraud from continuing? Focusing on education and increasing awareness among possible victims and law enforcement organizations is a crucial strategy. We may lessen the number of victims by informing people about the dangers of the Yahoo Yahoo scam and how to recognize its warning indications. To keep one step ahead of con artists, law enforcement organizations might endeavor to enhance their detection and response skills.

Another strategy is to concentrate on strengthening the financial system's security to make it more difficult for con artists to obtain payments and launder their money. This would entail making more use of blockchain technology, which can contribute to the development of a more transparent and secure financial system.

A multifaceted strategy incorporating education, technology, and collaboration between law enforcement agencies, financial institutions, and civil society organizations will ultimately be needed to battle the future of Yahoo Yahoo fraud. Together, we can assist to stop other individuals from falling for this terrible and harmful fraud.

Conclusion

In this book, we have investigated the growth of online fraud in Nigeria, from the early days of 419 to the advent of Yahoo Yahoo. We have explored the impact of online fraud on Nigerian society, the problems of prosecuting internet scammers, and the attempts of law enforcement to combat internet scams.

Online fraud has had a tremendously detrimental impact on individuals, organizations, and the reputation of Nigeria. The growth of Yahoo Yahoo and the development of online frauds have been driven by poverty, unemployment, and the fast advancement of technology.

However, we have also shown that education and awareness may play a key role in combating internet fraud. Public education programs, especially those focused on vulnerable populations, can assist individuals to avoid becoming victims of internet fraud.

Furthermore, we must continue to develop and implement measures to avoid the growth of internet fraud. This involves boosting the resources available to law enforcement authorities, improving international coordination, and creating new technology to identify and prevent online fraud.

In conclusion, the fight against online fraud in Nigeria is a constant battle, but by working together, we may continue to make progress in tackling this issue. It is our aim that this book has thrown light on the growth of internet scams in Nigeria and the measures to prevent their proliferation, ultimately contributing to a safer and more secure online environment for everyone.

www.ingramcontent.com/pod-product-compliance
Lightning Source LLC
Chambersburg PA
CBHW071130220526
45467CB00004B/2114